Access® 2021 & 365 Introduction

TEACHUCOMP, INC.®

AF731007

Quick Reference Guide

Comprehensive video training & instruction manuals available at www.teachucomp.com

About Access

Overview of a Database

Access is a "relational database" program. In a relational database, you store large amounts of data into the smallest possible increments within tables. You then relate these tables together by joining common fields between them. In this way, you store less redundant data and your database will operate more quickly and efficiently. When you relate tables, you are then able to access any data in the related tables. In Access, you manipulate a contained collection of smaller objects within a database file.

Access Definitions

Database: A collection of tables, queries, forms, reports, macros, and modules.
Datasheet View: Displays data from a table, form, query, view, or macro in a row-and-column format. Used to edit fields, add, delete, and search for data.
Design View: Used to create new database objects and modify the design of existing objects.
Field: A column of data or single piece of data.
Form: An object which uses controls to perform actions or to enter, display, and edit data in fields.
Macro: An action or actions that automate tasks.
Module: A collection of user-defined functions, subroutines, and global variables written in VBA code, which can be accessed from anywhere in the database.
Navigation Pane: Appears at left when you open an Access database. Displays objects in the database.
Query: A request for data results, for action on data, or both. A query can answer a simple question, perform calculations, combine data from different tables, and add, change, or delete table data.
Record: A row of data, made up of different fields.
Report: A printable object containing information formatted and organized according to specifications.
Table: A database object that stores data in records (rows) and fields (columns).

Access Basics

Creating a Database

1. **To create a new database**, click either the BLANK database thumbnail or a template thumbnail in the Startup Screen. *Or*, click the "File" tab in the Ribbon, select "New" from the menu at the left in Backstage View, and then select a thumbnail.
2. **To find online templates**, click a "Suggested searches" link or type in the "Search for Online Templates" text box and press "Enter" or click the "Start searching" button, then select a thumbnail.
3. Enter a name in the "File Name" field.
4. **To change the default location where the database is saved**, click the small folder button at the right end of the "File Name" field, navigate to the location, and click the "OK" button.
5. Click the "Create" button.

Creating a Table in Datasheet View

1. Click the "Table" button in the "Tables" group on the "Create" tab in the Ribbon.
2. Click the "Click to Add" heading, select a field type, enter the field name (64 max characters, no spaces), and press the "Enter" key. Repeat for each subsequent field that appears until all desired fields have been added.
3. Click the "File" tab in the Ribbon and choose "Save."
4. Type a table name, and click "OK."

To create a table from a template:

1. Click the "Application Parts" button in the "Templates" group on the "Create" tab in the Ribbon.
2. Select a "Quick Start" item, then follow the wizard.

Switching Between Object Views

1. **To open an object (table, query, form, report, etc.)**, double-click it in the Navigation Pane.
2. Click the drop-down arrow at the bottom of the "View" button in the "Views" group on the "Home" tab in the Ribbon and select a view. ***Or*, to toggle views**, click the upper-portion of the button instead.

Datasheet View

Entering and Editing Table Data

To add a record:

1. Click into the first field in the empty row at the bottom of the table. *Or*, click the "New (blank) record" button in the lower-left corner of the table.
2. Type data into the first field. **To advance to the next field**, press the "Enter" or "Tab" key. Repeat for each field. **To advance to a new record**, press the "Enter" or "Tab" key in the last field of the record.

To edit a record:

1. Click into the field of the record and make desired edits using normal word processing techniques. A pencil icon appears in the row's selector box at the left end of the row to indicate unsaved changes.
2. Exit the field. Access automatically saves changes.

To delete a record:

1. Click the row selector at the far left end of the row to select the entire record. A border will appear around the entire row.
2. Press the "Delete" key. *Or*, click the "Delete" button in the "Records" group on the "Home" tab in the Ribbon. Click "Yes" to confirm the deletion.

Sorting Table Data

1. Click the drop-down arrow to the right of the field heading. *Or*, right-click in the field to sort by.
2. Choose "Sort A to Z" or "Sort Z to A."

Navigating in Datasheet View

1. **To move up, down, left or right through the data**, use the arrow keys on your keyboard.
2. **To move to the right through the fields**, press the "Tab" or "Enter" keys on your keyboard.
3. **To move to the left through the fields**, press the "Shift" + "Tab" keys on your keyboard.
4. **To scroll through the records**, use the horizontal and vertical scroll bars in the datasheet view.
5. **To move to a designated record**, click the "First Record," "Previous Record," "Next Record," or "Last Record" button in the "Record" button group in the lower-left corner.
6. **To jump to a specific record**, enter the record number in the "Current Record" field within the "Record" button group and press the "Enter" key.

Searching for a Record

1. Click into the desired field.
2. Click the "Find" button in the "Find" group on the "Home" Tab in the Ribbon. ***Or***, press "Ctrl" + "F".
3. Type the data to search for in the "Find What" field.
4. **To search for data in more than one field**, select "Current document" from the "Look In" drop-down.
5. **To search for a portion of a word or field**, select a choice from the "Match" drop-down.
6. **To change the direction of the search from the current location in the table**, change the "Search" drop-down to "Up," "Down," or "All."
7. Click the "Find Next" button. Repeat as desired.
8. Click "Cancel" when done.

Data Entry Shortcuts

Enter Current Date	**CTRL + ; (semicolon)**
Enter Current Time	**CTRL + : (colon)**
Copy from previous record into current field	**CTRL + ' (apostrophe)**

Primary

Assigning

A primary key in a relational database is a field (column) or combination of fields that produces a unique identifier for each record in a table. The primary key prevents duplicate records from being created and is used to establish and maintain the relationship between tables or within queries. It can be a normal attribute that is guaranteed to be unique such as a Social Security number. If no unique information exists, a primary key such as the default field "ID" (automatically generated when creating tables in Datasheet View) can be used. It is through the primary key assignment that you create the necessary relationships between data tables, eliminating redundant information. For example, you may have one table for "Customers," one table for "Items," and a third for "Orders." A single customer may produce many different orders. A "Customer_ID" primary key can be used so that the customer only occupies a single row in the "Customers" table, but is associated with several orders in the "Orders" table.

To assign or remove a Primary Key:

1. Open the table in Design View.
2. Click into the desired field.
3. **To toggle the Primary Key "On" or "Off,"** click the "Primary Key" button in the "Tools" group on the "Table Design" contextual tab in the Ribbon.

Joining Tables

A relationship between tables allows you to access information from them through their "shared" or "common" fields by which they are joined. Relationships between tables are created in the "Relationships" window, where the tables are added. To join tables together, they must have shared fields.

1. Click the "Relationships" button in the "Relationships" group on the "Database Tools" tab in the Ribbon.
2. **To launch the "Add Tables" pane**, click the "Add Tables" button in the "Relationships" group on the "Relationships Design" tab, if necessary.
3. Select the tables on the "Tables" tab and click "Add Selected Tables."
4. Click "Close" when done adding tables.
5. Click and drag the field from one table window and drop it on the shared field of the other table.
6. Check desired "Referential Integrity" options.
7. Click the "Join Type" button, select a type, click "OK."
8. Click the "Create" button.
9. Click the "File" tab in the Ribbon and select "Save."
10. Click the "Close" button in the "Relationships" group on the "Relationships Design" tab.

Editing and Deleting Table Joins

To edit a table join, open the Relationships window:

1. Double-click the join that you want to edit.
2. Make desired changes and click "OK."
3. Click the "File" tab in the Ribbon and select "Save."
4. Click the "Close" button.

To delete a join, open the Relationships window:

1. Click the join that you want to delete.
2. Press the "Delete" button. Click "Yes" to confirm.
3. Click the "File" tab in the Ribbon and select "Save."
4. Click the "Close" button.

TeachUcomp, Inc.
Computer Software Training & Continuing Education.
www.teachucomp.com
info@teachucomp.com
877.925.8080

Modifying Tables in Design View

Use Design View to modify tables. **To quickly open a table in Design View**, select the table in the Navigation Pane, then press the "Ctrl" + "Enter" keys.

Inserting New Table Fields

1. Open the table in Design View.
2. Click the row selector of the row above which you wish to insert the new field.
3. Click the "Insert Rows" button in the "Tools" group on the "Table Design" tab in the Ribbon. Insert Rows
4. Click into "Field Name," and type a name.
5. Select a data type from the "Data Type" drop-down.
6. Enter a description in the "Description" column.
7. Click the "File" tab in the Ribbon and select "Save."

Renaming Table Fields

1. Open the table in Design View.
2. Click into "Field Name," and type a name.
3. Click the "File" tab in the Ribbon and select "Save."

Deleting Table Fields

1. Open the table in Design View.
2. Click the row selector of the row to delete.
3. Click the "Delete Rows" button in the "Tools" group on the "Table Design" tab in the Ribbon. Delete Rows
4. Click "Yes" to delete the field and all of its data.
5. Click the "File" tab in the Ribbon and select "Save."

Setting Table Field Properties

Table field properties are set in Design View. Available properties (size, format, alignment, input mask, etc.) are determined by the field data type. For example, "Decimal Places" is available for number and currency fields, but not others such as text fields. Click into a property in the "Field Properties" section at the bottom of the Design View window to view a description of the property to the right of the grid.

1. Open the table in Design View.
2. Select the field in the design grid.
3. In the "Field Properties" section at the bottom of the window, select the "General" tab.
4. Click into a field property and enter a value or use the drop-down menu or "Expression Builder" button at the far-right end of the property box.
5. Click the "File" tab in the Ribbon and select "Save."

Queries

Creating and Modifying Queries

1. **To create a new query**, click the "Query Design" button in the "Queries" group on the "Create" tab in the Ribbon. ***Or*, to modify an existing query**, right-click the query in the Navigation Pane and select "Design View." Query Design
2. If the "Add Tables" pane does not appear, click the "Add Tables" button in the "Query Setup" group on the "Query Design" tab in the Ribbon. Add Tables
3. Click the "Tables" tab in the "Add Tables" pane, select a table, and click "Add Selected Tables." Repeat as necessary.
4. Click the "Close" button in the "Add Tables" pane.
5. Select the first field to add to the query by clicking and dragging the field from the table shown, and dropping it into the "Field" row of the lower query grid. Repeat for any other desired fields.
6. Make selections in the "Sort," "Show," and "Criteria" rows of the lower query grid.
   Sort: Creates sorted results.
   Show: Determines which fields will be displayed. For example, you may not wish to display a field only used for sorting.
   Criteria: Specifies which records will be displayed.
7. Click the "File" tab in the Ribbon and select "Save."
8. Enter a query name and click "OK."

Query Grid Criteria

Dates: Type the date in short format surrounded by number signs (#). ***Example***: #2/10/22# matches February 10, 2022. **To define a date range**, use **Between...and.** ***Example***: Between #2/10/19# And #3/10/19# to search February 10 to March 10, 2019.

Empty Data: **To find empty data**, use **Is Null**. Use **Is Not Null** for non-empty data.

Numbers: Enter the number alone (***example***: 2) ***or*** with comparison modifiers (***example***: <10):

>	Greater than
>=	Greater than or equal to
<	Less than
<=	Less than or equal to
=	Equal to
<>	Does not equal

Text: Type the text to match surrounded by double quotes ("). **To refine the text search**:

Use	To	Example
OR	Match more than one possible entry	"Blue" or "Green"
NOT	Exclude a word	NOT "Blue"
LIKE	Match using wildcards:	
?	Match single unknown unknown character	LIKE "?lue" returns Blue, Glue, Clue, etc.
*	Match multiple unknown characters	LIKE "Bl*" returns Blue, Black, Blast, etc.

Note: The placement of the asterisk determines which part of the phrase is matched (before, after, or middle).
Example: LIKE "*bl" returns records *ending* with bl.
LIKE "*Bl*" returns **Bl**ue, Ta**bl**e, Tum**bl**e, etc.

Running a Query

To run a query and display the results in Datasheet View, double-click the query in the Navigation Pane. *Or*, in Design View, click the "Run" button in the "Results" group on the "Query Design" tab in the Ribbon. Run

Forms

Creating and Modifying Forms

1. Select a table or query in the Navigation Pane.
2. Click the "More Forms" drop-down button in the "Forms" group on the "Create" tab in the Ribbon.
3. Select a form type from the list: More Forms
   Multiple Items: Displays multiple table records in the form, with each record displayed in its own row.
   Datasheet: Operates in the exact same way as the "Datasheet" view of a table.
   Split Form: Shows the currently selected record from the underlying data source at the top and an accompanying "Datasheet View" at the bottom.
   Modal Dialog: No data source. Forces a user to respond (e.g. "OK" or "Cancel") before continuing.
4. **To modify the layout in layout or design view**, click and drag the field labels and data placeholders to change their position and size.
5. Click the "File" tab in the Ribbon and select "Save."
6. Enter a form name and click "OK."

Using the Form Wizard

1. Click the "Form Wizard" button in the "Forms" group on the "Create" tab in the Ribbon. Form Wizard
2. **To add a field**, click to select it in the "Available Fields" list and click the "Add" button. >
   Repeat as necessary. ***Or*, to add all fields**, click the "Add All" button. >> **To remove a field**, select it in the "Selected Fields" list and click "Remove." <
   ***Or*, to remove all fields**, click the "Remove All" button. << Click the "Next" button.
3. Select a form type and click "Next":
   Columnar: Multi-column. Displays one record at a time.
   Tabular: One row per record. Displays multiple records.
   Datasheet: Spreadsheet-style display.
   Justified: Multiple fields justified to a common width.
4. Enter a form name and click "Finish."
5. Click the "File" tab in the Ribbon and select "Save."

Reports

Creating and Modifying Reports

1. Select the table or query in the Navigation Pane on which to base the report.
2. Click the "Report" button in the "Reports" group on the "Create" tab in the Ribbon. ***Or*, to modify an existing report**, right-click the report in the Navigation Pane and select "Layout View." Report
3. Access automatically creates a simple report that can be used to display the selected information.
4. **To modify the report**, click elements within the form and use the various settings on the "Report Layout Design," "Arrange," "Format," and "Page Setup" tabs in the Ribbon:
   Report Layout Design: Assign themes, group and sort, insert controls, set headers and footers, etc.
   Arrange: Arrange fields within the form.
   Format: Adjust fonts, numbering, backgrounds, and control formatting.
   Page Setup: Adjust page size, margins, and page layout.
5. Click the "File" tab in the Ribbon and select "Save."
6. Enter a report name and click "OK," if necessary.

Using the Report Wizard

1. Click the "Report Wizard" button in the "Reports" group on the "Create" tab in the Ribbon. Report Wizard
2. Select the main table or query on which to base the report from the "Tables/Queries" drop-down.
3. **To add a field**, click to select it in the "Available Fields" list and click the "Add" button. >
   Repeat as necessary. ***Or*, to add all fields**, click the "Add All" button. >> **To remove a field**, select it in the "Selected Fields" list and click "Remove." <
   ***Or*, to remove all fields**, click the "Remove All" button. << Click the "Next" button.
4. Select any fields by which to group the data, and click the "Add" button to add them to the report. >
   To remove any of the groups or change their priority, click to select it and click the "Remove" < button or the "Priority" buttons.
5. **To customize grouping**, click the "Grouping Options" button, make selections, and click "OK."
6. Click the "Next" button.
7. Select up to four levels of sorting and sorting options. **To add totals and subtotals**, click the "Summary Options" button, if available. Click "Next."
8. Select layout and orientation options. Click "Next."
9. Enter a report name and click "Finish."
10. **To adjust page and print settings**, make selections in the "Print Preview" Ribbon.
11. **To export the report**, click the "Excel" button in the "Data" group in the Ribbon, or select the "More" button and an export option from the list, select a location to save the report. Click "OK."
12. Click the "Close Print Preview" button in the Ribbon.
13. Click the "File" tab in the Ribbon and select "Save."

Printing Reports

1. Double-click the report in the Navigation Pane.
2. **To zoom in or out, or adjust print settings**, click the "View" button in the "Views" group on the "Home" tab in the Ribbon and select "Print Preview" from the drop-down. Click the "Close Print Preview" button in the Ribbon when done. View
3. **To print**, click the "File" tab in the Ribbon and then the "Print" command in the menu to the left.
4. **To immediately print a single copy of the report**, click the "Quick Print" command to the right. ***Or*, to select a printer, number of copies, and other print options**, click the "Print" command to the right, adjust settings, and click "OK."

ISBN 978-1-941854-83-9